Presented in honor of your
outstanding achievement in the
Arts & Writing Contest of

THE SANDRA BORNSTEIN HOLOCAUST EDUCATION CENTER

By the Dr. Alfred Jaffe
Endowment Fund

Crossing the Stream

POEMS BY

Laura Chakrin Cable

Cover photo: Ava Wolf

Design: Lisa Wolf

Printed by RPI Printing, Fall River, Massachusetts, USA

Acknowledgements

To the 'writer's group,' Ava Wolf, Diane Gnepp, and Mara Sokolsky, who with Judy Semonoff spent countless hours sorting and deciding, reading and re-reading, lighting candles and praying; all the time struggling to remain faithful and connected to Laura, and to the intention of her work.

To Lisa Wolf for her sensivity, creativity, and skill in laying out the book and developing its cover.

To Anna, whose spirit carries with it the insight, empathy and love that is her mother's legacy.

And to Adam, who strove to protect the sacred nature of his mother's work.

DEDICATION

This is for my friends who've carried me through
If it weren't for you
If it weren't for you

You came to my door with a flower a book
A wish and a look
that said I could cry or laugh or even die
And if I did you would be there
to carry me through
This is for you.

Laura Chakrin Cable

TABLE OF CONTENTS

Acknowledgements I

Dedication III

Foreword 1

Wanting Daddy 7

Mama 8

After the Wedding .10

Being Saved 11

The Voyage 13

House Hunting 15

My Newborn 16

Why Is It Women .17

It's the Odd Times 18

Displaced Persons .19

Then There Was No Praise 21

Beckoned from Harbor to Sea Mist 23

At the JCC Playground with Adam 24

The Trees of Poland 25

The Candles Wait .26

A Second Art 27

Simchas Torah 1993 28

Your Granddaughter is 13 30

Euthanasia for Tiger 32

After Holocaust Memorial Dedication 34

Dear Editor 35

Crossing the Stream 36

Mama in the Hospital 38

Lot's Wife and her Descendant Ruth 39

Making Shabbos in the Line of Fire 40

We Write Poetry Together 42

Mom at the Chanukah Party 43

Remembrance for Mom 44

Shiva 45

High School Graduate 46

Large 48

Sunday June 22, 1997 49

My Father Aaron's Words 51

The Fire in Rob's Office 53

Cancer with Community 54

The Alexander Lesson After Auschwitz 55

Biological Clock 9/30/02 56

Biological Clock 11/26/02 57

My Feet 58

Shore's Edge 59

Underground 61

Stage IV Breast Cancer 63

Transferring Eddie's Hours 64

Bone Box 65

For Sue on Losing Don 66

Post Diagnosis 67

Afterword 69

FOREWORD

Laura Chakrin Cable wished she had more time to write. The story goes that Jane Austen wrote her novels in her spare moments, hiding her words beneath doilies between times, while playing her part at social events in her father's house. Laura also took the opportunity to write her poems whenever she could in the midst of a busy and demanding personal

and professional life, often writing on scraps of paper, or the backs of notices for lectures scheduled for therapists.

She often spoke of sorting through all her poems with an eye toward sending some of them out into the world, and all of us had offered to support her in such an endeavor. In *Post Diagnosis*, Laura says of her poems, "and I cast up my

Laura at Masada in Israel.

nets to collect them before I die." Time ran out. But Laura's subtle and powerful personality magnetized people to her. As it turned out, our writing group was unwittingly, yet willingly, caught up in Laura's nets of intelligence, humor, and compassion. So it fell to us to collect her poems after her death.

We did not know how to begin our task of sorting the contents of two shopping bags her husband Rob filled with Laura's writings. We began with light. Two candles were placed in lovely glass candlesticks, and just as we would welcome the Sabbath bride on Friday night, we welcomed Laura's spirit to guide us.

We scooped up a pile of Laura's heart-filled words; one of us would read what was on the page. Silence followed. Tears, remembrance, laughter, amazement and gratitude filled the room. More silence. From that fertile place a consensus was reached. The poem was then placed into its proper folder: yes, no, maybe.

It's true that Laura knew some of the most disturbing and distressing experiences which a person can face—some firsthand, some by her inheritance as the child of Holocaust survivors. Through her poems we got a glimpse of their impact. Laura was reluctant to share these poems with her family and friends. As her son Adam articulated, "I think she felt that I would be too overwhelmed by the range and intensity of her writing. She did not hold anything back from her poems. My mother's writing is a true and clear window into her existence." But despite her reluctance to share the poems, Laura had a need to express her legacy of loss. Her poetry was perhaps one way to reconcile this legacy with the everyday blessings that surrounded her.

Still, *im kol zeh*—with all of this, we remember Laura as a woman who loved life, not with a naïve love, but with a love that acknowledged human flaws, pain, and the capacity for evil. As we read, we remember what the poems may not reveal: the sound of her giggle, how easily it came and how infectious it was; her ability to laugh at the absurdities of life; the way she made her friends, her family, and her clients feel so safe in her presence.

The process has taken us nine months. Poems typed, order established, photos selected. Our task changed from being the gatherers left on shore to the releasers of Laura's light.

Diane, Mara, Judy, Ava

*Laura's paternal grandmother
and family.*

Laura's maternal grandparents and family.

CROSSING THE STREAM

POEMS BY

LAURA CHAKRIN CABLE

Wanting Daddy

Once upon a time
on gloomy days
when moments ticked like metronomes
in old gray rooms
I looked for you.

I pulled the box from the hall linen closet
where it lay buried by frayed linens
and dragged you to my room
to dream—
to be held little on your lap.

I searched through files of old notebooks
with algebraic equations
and the carbons of correspondence
the doodles and notes

your papers opened like outstretched arms,
embracing my aching
absorbing my tears
as if you were there,
drying my eyes
and stroking my hair.

I watched those tears melt into the paper,
staining and warping and yearning to touch you
and leave their mark.

I studied each page, as if in prayer
pleading with fate I'd find the way
to bring you to flesh
until the silence of the lines
pressed on my chest and I feared
pain and death so the books fell,
and I wept, alone again,
with the metronome striking me
endlessly. ✎

Mama

I always knew
when I grew big
I'd make it up to you.

I took the ripped photo from the drawer
I brought back more, restored,
and in those frames
are held the faces
that gaze so steadily
on all my days

I dreamed how someday
I would fill
all the holes
so completely
the traces of scars
would be
all gone

And now the wound
that cuts me deepest
is being big
and so gone from you

All the A's
degrees,
even chubby babies
don't make up
for the terror
the horror
the broken life

And in the course
of getting big
I too
left you
alone

I ache for you
I ache to heal you
and to know
I cannot
I ache for your blessing
with my words so foreign
to your mother tongue

I weep to see
that in getting big
I too
left you
alone,
as I too
am left
alone. ❧

AFTER THE WEDDING

After the wedding—
    amid the torn papers
    bright boxes

Still-fresh impressions
    fresh as flowers...

The nervousness,
    the dreamy feeling of walking
    past the faces that smiled

So many smiles—
    the energy that jolted the air,
    the sadness of brief connections,
    or unspoken knots—

The celebration
    of love, hope, faithfulness
    all we aspire to—

Friendships that have sustained
    through wanderings,
    distances
    disappointments—

To come together
    to sing praise to the Lord
    and our lives. ✍

BEING SAVED

That giddy noon
I swam from shore
toward the end of earth
and the start of heaven.

I savored and thrilled
to surpass the known!
Gliding through liquid
light, till with no warning
I dropped down
deep, in an undertow
that seized my breath

and heaved me only
to briefly see that happy
beach, its umbrellas
rejoicing, its bathers
content, and then, again,
the madness devoured me,
spewed me, over and over.

It teased me, let me see
my beloved searching
the sea. But I, mute,
only sucked and spit
until my spirit was swallowed
and I surrendered, slid down,
down, through the ocean's
smooth throat, seduced
by the ease of sinking
and the water's song:
"Release, release,
and freely breathe!"
Till my wasted body
wilted, waited, and

Disbelieved the reach
of those arms embracing
my shoulders and towing me
in, in through the wetness
that bitterly yielded me
onto the beach, the velvet
sand beneath me,
my beloved's gaze and
relief, the softest towel
enfolding me: dry,
dry, destined to live. ✑

The Voyage

When I was 22 I needed to see
another piece of the globe. So I fled
New York and flew to the Congo,

Visiting heaven along the way,
gazing at the various shapes of water
from my window in the sky.

I landed, boarded trucks and boats
down rivers, into ports, arrived
in the village where I would stay.

And under the same heaven
that still embraced home,
I learned new words and work.

At the Centre for Nutrition
I sat with the skeletal mother
and her hollow-bellied daughter.

Ghostlike, she banged at the manioc,
despite knowing she could not defeat
her uncles' curse. She died.

Daily I gaped at the women along my way:
vast basins of flour and water balanced
on their heads, as if weightless as air,

or justice. They laughed at me,
White as powdered milk in cans
sold by Americans. I could not

lift the basin to my head
with any luck or grace,
I had no children on my back.

Amused they called out incessantly,
"How many children do you have?"
"Ten!" I would joke.
They yelled, "Where are they?"

I learned about same and other:
eyes as brown as mine,
teeth that smiled in a foreign language,
women expected to be dead by forty.

I missed home, and blending in,
and my mother's cooking.
I flew back.

To fully stocked store shelves, electricity,
cereal sold in predictably sized boxes
I could carry in my arms.

And now, years later, in my new kitchen
in New England, I push one button
for filtered water, another for crushed ice.

I savor the time with my daughter, 17,
beside me, chopping carrots, stirring soup.
The light seems to nod its blessing. ❧

HOUSEHUNTING

These homes on American Dream Street beckon
to their gardens and glowing doorways
like Vegas girls lifting their skirts
and whispering their prices

Dick and Jane smirk from their shuttered windows
They watch us walk in and out
wanting that Good Life
unable to buy it, it seems.
Our hopes like wrinkled skin
of African mothers' breasts
folded over promises
pleading with fate.

In America we grieve for glitter
wounded and starved
with enough. ❧

My Newborn, Years After the Holocaust

Your quivers and cries beckon
my milk to fill your hunger
and my arms
to hold you close

Your eyes as wide
as my sorrow
to recall those mothers
whose babies beseeched

them for comfort and nurture
before the eyes
of the killers. ❧

WHY IS IT WOMEN WHO ALWAYS LOSE THEIR VOICES?

I lost my voice
beneath stacks of bills
or in the corner of my underwear drawer
between the hiking socks
and the nursing bra.
My voice disappeared into the black hole.
Sometimes I hear traces of it
in my children's words
mixed with their father's. ❧

IT'S THE ODD TIMES

It's the odd times
thoughts drift in like gas
from a showerhead
on a lazy morning

Unwrapping chocolate
for my child's sweet treat
or buying shoes
for growing feet

Or teaching not to stomp
on ants
or writing their names on toys
to be returned

Ugly smells curl out
from safe-looking places
like gas from the showerhead
on a lazy Sunday morning

Drifting, sticking
mocking the notion
we can plan. ❧

DISPLACED PERSONS

I read the ad in the Survivors' newspaper:
An urgent call for artifacts of the war,
an exhibit on the untold story of Displaced
Persons. It seemed only right to send a note,
offering my parents' photos, notebooks,
boarding passes, identity cards. All had once
    been hidden

in my mother's dresser. Underneath underwear,
    hidden
from my girlish eyes. Over time, I'd found them:
    folded paper
upon paper in Russian, German; Disjointed
    writing in books
in Polish, Yiddish, English: records of war.
Departures, arrivals, passes: my parents' notes.
I had cleaned out the apartment, and placed

them for safekeeping in my own secret place.
My heirlooms, after all: jewels, hidden
from dust and thieves and casual note.
My parents had died and left me papers.
Someday I would translate the war into words
I could understand. Someday I would read the book

kept by my father, his neat columns of record books
of vocational training at a Displaced
Persons' Camp in Munich. After the war,
my parents met there. My mother had been hidden,
found, beaten, jailed, escaped, lived on false papers.
His survival a mystery, he taught her English
    and took note

of her beauty. They married, though no note
of who witnessed this. No family. No feast.
   No guestbook.
Decades later, the curator arrived to examine
   the papers.
Despite my sweaty search, I was forced to
   confess: I'd misplaced
everything. All that evidence vanished.
   Apparently hidden.
He sat politely on the couch. I mumbled words

of apology. He departed, with his own
   puzzled words,
left a business card in case things of note
reemerged. More months passed, with all
   still hidden,
the exhibit opened, reviews appeared in books.
Then on Rosh Hashanah, I hunted my drawers
   for place
mats and there appeared my parents' papers.

I sent no note to the curator. I kept all
   the papers.
I still cannot comprehend the words, the war,
   the books.
But day by day, I retrieve what is hidden, and
   invent my place. ✎

THEN THERE WAS NO PRAISE

Then
there was
no praise,
no parades

no medals
no monuments
only eyes
that looked away
too busy or bored
above such grime
of grim misfortune
wearing their fate like furs
as if they'd been earned

Greeted instead
by the void;
the voices of the dead;
the barks and gunshots
that chase you still
through night
and day;
the ache for home
for what should have been;
the scars of evils
you buried with silence

You survived
and so much more: spitting on the pity
of the lucky
who wore their fortune
like furs as if they'd earned it;
your pride, unlike theirs,
was forged by fate

You worked
you paid
you clothed
and fed
through days and weeks
and seasons and years
without parents
and brothers
to see you through
to drink your wine
to see your babies
to see your homes
and we became
ourselves
through you

How I pray:
through us
might you be
redeemed

We, and our children,
are the living memorial
we would weep your tears,
would breathe your sighs,
would tell your tales
if only it would lift
the weight of your pain. ❧

Beckoned From Harbor to Sea Mist

Beckoned from harbor to sea mist
I leave you
rocking on ocean and blanketed with fog
lulled by the boat motor
waiting for land
my dreaminess pierced by the horn
frazzled by the chatter

I hold your image in my mind
like a Buddhist praying
for home. ❧

At the JCC Playground with Adam
On the Second Anniversary of the Holocaust Memorial

My little boy
crusades up mountains
careens down slides
brandishing swords
to slay evil ones

    From gray rock there
    the birds fly to see

    Lamentation behind laughter
    Pride washed with grief
    Fly back birds
    Fly back, I plead
    Carry this to the lost ones:
    We are here
      they are here
    We remember
      Every day. ❧

THE TREES OF POLAND

They rise above those killing fields
moaning in spaces
between the leaves

Chorus to the grass that weaves
a quilt, a cloak
to what lays below
Children, God's holiness,
overthrown.

Trees that betrayed
their noble promise
Never lunged on killers' backs
Never laid pathways for mothers' escape

Instead they stood
in daylight, mute,
as if all was
how it should have been.

Now they groan
with endless ache
Of babies' blood
And brood beneath serene veneer
they sway in shame
in tortured prayer. ❧

THE CANDLES WAIT

The candles wait
On the mantle,
watched by the photo
of my family.
They summon me
to our weekly trial.
I come but wear jeans
and sneakers and
let children watch tv
nearby.

The candles wait,
erect and patient as guards
who know I will eventually
arrive.

They stand like chimneys
like barrels of rifles
that killed her.

She, whose name I bear,
whose soul breathes still
through these parched lips

Who waits now too
for me to make Shabbos
as she did then
each time
until

I yearn for her faith
but questions rise
like smoke from me

Where was he,
this King who demands
His due? ❧

A Second Art

The art of losing brings a guest in tow,
incognito, who teaches another art: to find;
to name your needs, what you need to know.

Let's say your car was stolen a moment ago.
You discover the cop is actually kind.
The art of losing brings a guest in tow.

Or say your lover left you. The birds fly slow,
The pictures are tilted, the stars misaligned.
To name your needs, what you need to know

is new. You allow an old friend to drag you
    to a show.
You laugh, though you thought you'd left
    laughter behind.
The art of losing brings a guest in tow.

To fight the void you plant tomatoes. After weeks
    they grow!
You find yourself delighted to share them with the
    widow confined.
To name your needs, what you need to know

is to seek words and music that lift you from low,
from before, into light, in ways newly designed.
The art of losing brings a guest in tow,
to name your needs, what you need to know. ❧

SIMCHAS TORAH 1993

The vapor arrives
when I forget to remember.
While preparing the family
for Simchas Torah at Temple,
I shower
and choke on Shoah.

Later we all walk through the night
towards simcha.
My daughter's small fingers tighten on mine
as she asks in a chilly whisper
if there's a monster in the dark.
I yearn to comfort more
but my breath is haunted
by aches and echoes.

We are lucky.
Her father reassures:
We are safe.

At Temple
the congregants dance
as if flying on air
as if nothing to fear.
Is it only for me
that all joy sheds tears
for the ones taken then
and absent today
from all joy?

Later at home
my son savors his treat:
"<u>M</u>y cookie!" he smiles.
I savor his safety
yet crumble inside
for the mothers
who could not keep
the sweets for their children,
who could not keep
the monsters away. ✦

Your Granddaughter is Thirteen
For Mama

I meet you in the mirror each morning
smoothing lotion in my skin
line denying, age defying
circling upward as we learned
in the Woman's magazine
when I was thirteen.
Thirsty skin around my eyes
drinks in milky softness,
as you advised me
it would.

Me little,
sitting on the wobbly toilet seat,
a perfect view,
of you leaning against the sink
eyes pressed close to the mirror,
lining your eyebrows.
Tall and majestic
knowing just how to draw your lips
and kiss the tissue so they set
right.

I see your brown eyes
embrace me, saying
"I miss you too."
I recall that evening in hospital
in the bed by the window.
I rolled you the way they showed me.
You gripped the rail,
Suddenly stopped tugging and turning,
You saw me; a smile lit your eyes
"Such a pretty face!"
and weariness slipped off me
like old skin.

I watch along with you
as Anna learns the moves
smiling in the mirror
smoothing her hair
When it's time, I'll show her
Eterna 27, just the way
you would want me to do.

EUTHANASIA
FOR TIGER

The assistant escorted us to the snack room,
my son and daughter, and Tiger in her pet taxi
with the sign "Warning Live Animals Inside".
We placed her on the metal table and opened the cage
but she clung to the inside
and purred when we pet her.

We waited, and as the minutes accused us
noticed the fridge and hot chocolate
and chocolate chip cookies on the shelf
beneath the tv

I turned it on,
wanting Oprah and gossip
to take me away.
Anna scolded me
with teenage righteousness
but I wanted the time to race,
not blame me, empty inch by inch.

Finally the pet doctor entered,
frowned when I asked if Anna could hold Tiger,
then agreed to try.

The assistant got her out of the cage,
"Come on sweetie, it will be okay"
and put her on Anna's lap.
He shaved her paw and filled the needle and
    squeezed it into her body
"Is that the sedative?" I asked.
"No, she's gone."

It's so easy to kill.
If you just saw this
you'd never know
how hard it is
to keep alive
cats and children and dreams. ∽

AFTER HOLOCAUST MEMORIAL DEDICATION

Why is it I weep
when the springtime comes?
I mourn to see the blossoms born
As if I was witnessing wilting.

Winter gone;
I grieve,
As if cold had triumphed,
claimed spoils,
and departed forever
with its catch.

While I am left standing,
staring, alone,
surrounded by newborns
who do not know
whose places
they have taken. ❧

Dear Editor

Enclosed is no poem for your review.
After careful consideration I
have concluded that I will not submit
my offspring to the risk of dismissal.
I would not sleep to think its words crumpled
in the trash with other silenced leaves, and
I too far to soothe its bruised skin.
When, in a minute, or a year, it matures,
and its voice can holler from any heap:
"I will not submit!"

Then, dear Editor,
I will submit, and transcend with grace
Your disdain, indifference, or embrace. ❧

CROSSING THE STREAM
In Shenandoah, Virginia

I step on rocks to reach the other side.
corpses swim beneath me,
the blood of aunts uncles cousins grandparents.

Sunlight brilliant on water
like plundered jewels.
not diamonds and golden teeth;
true gems:
my kin
my parents' youth
lives of quiet delight.

These cold gray slabs look large enough to hold me.
Some are; some shake, startle;
I consider choices and what awaits:

Forest green with old oak trees
apathetic sun shining, as on death marches—
children fell like twigs now sleeping in the bushes—
Bitter snakes rattle their tongues,
Daring: Enjoy your hike!

The stream thrusts onward,
throwing water
eternally.

Spirits sing
in sadness, inside me, incessantly—
Remember us!
Don't drown!
    in blood
    in bitterness
Delight!
    in the forest
    in our memory
You will find a true path!

The Earth sobs.
My boots cling to stones.
I pray for cleansing,
purity of purpose;
I cross the stream. ❧

MAMA IN THE HOSPITAL

Sunday morning while Mom phoned my brother
crying, from Room 226,
asking where she was,
and why

> hair matted, dried blood,
> over gash and staples
> she could not see

I wiped her kitchen counter.
Muddy teabag in a Yahrzeit glass,

> a box of fancy glasses
> waiting in the bedroom closet
> never opened.

Our lives are marked
by which empty spaces we fill
with what,
and how we fill them. ❧

Lot's Wife
and her descendant Ruth

looking back I always am
looking back at the void
that led to excess

my failure to speak
that announced my failure
to protect my girls,
my world. It did not matter

that years before another
man had offered me up,
or that I look back too,
on that, the line of women

who followed their men
one place and another.

wherever my legs
would have traveled
still I would have looked
back at what might have been,

the tears stopped me,
wrapped my legs and breath,
recalling the four girls
as babies, their voices

before the betrayals.
Redeemed only by the daughter of my daughter
who would follow another
kind of mother. ✎

Making Shabbos, In The Line of Fire
For My Grandmother

Once weekly, you will me your lifelines:
Wicks, wrapped in wax,
wait for light.

>*You tumbled in the pit*
>*your last strength wrapped around*
>*your youngest son*
>*to shield him from*
>*another mother's son*
>*who pulled the trigger*

I hear your prayer
to let myself be led
to link myself to you
to let my breathing blend
into the blessing

>*Blessed art Thou*
>*Lord our G-d*
>*Ruler of the Universe*
>*Who has sanctified us*
>*With your mitzvoth*
>*And commanded us*
>*To light the candles of Shabbat*

Light trembles
yet leaves no doubt where it points
to a better place than this,
a secret you cannot reveal
only a whisper
to do what you did,
and again next week,
and again, after that.

May I be undisturbed by sadness, by sorrow,
By sighing during the holy hours of Shabbat
Fill your servant's heart with joy, for to you,
O Lord, I offer my entire being.

Joy is lightness deeper than cheer
born of burden and fear
and heat that heals a broken soul.
A lullaby, a promise:
Rest, it is allowed
Endure, and strength will come
Tomorrow. ❧

We Write Poetry Together

We write poetry together
me and my clients
As the hours ski by outside my window
each arrives
in various shades of hope and hurt and horror.

We talk, we wait for words,
the wrong ones and the right ones
we revise them
and try new ones. ❧

MOM AT THE CHANUKAH PARTY

Your soul unfettered at last
set free from memories
of all those things
that should not be

After the singing you sat
admired the table
set with crystal and china
dark brown chocolates
luscious in their foils
sweet thin cakes flaunting
their beauty
on the silver trays

"What a spread!"
you could see now,
say again and again
"What a spread!"
your eyes delighting,
your cheeks now soft with ease
"What a spread!" ⤸

REMEMBRANCE
For Mama

I dreamt you went walking.
I waited and watched the clock
as worry edged to dread.

I remembered you'd forget your way home,
your bones would weep
your eyes would peer through veils of leaving.

The clock's hands moved, reluctant
as a mother knotting the bonnet
of a child she must give up.

The moments mounted, still no you.
My fingers pierced through a fog
to find a phone to call the police.

Then my eyes jolted open
and I exhaled:
Ahhhh…a nightmare

But memory assaulted,
insisted:
you had died

I knew there was an error.
I must see you again.

Then memory cradled,
comforted:

You had lain here,
in the sky blue room blessed by sunlight
waking in instants from that last long sleep
to gaze at us with fuzzy eyes.

You had let us love you
here, home, before you passed on. ✎

SHIVA

Friends held me end to end
I sat down and they entered and opened their
    books and prayed
I stood up, now the Mourner's words took my
    voice and there they were.
the words and the friends in the room
    the same room where brown oozed out of
    Mommy's mouth
for hours on end

breath gurgling, as books and nurses foretold, a
    death rattle,
til Bobby prayed for G-d to take her.

Her face the same one that smiled at the babies
    and the cameras
now we soothed it best we could with the softest
    cloths in the house,
and dried her mouth and prayed her sleep was
    deep enough she didn't know anything
except that we loved her inside our hearts if only
    we could have

held her thinning body inside ours we
    would have
she should have been on a cruise, a cool breeze
    softening sunlight
and family all around a summer holiday
instead she lay dying but if love counts she was
    rich, so rich, so held. ❧

High School Graduate

I don't want you to drive
on highways, fast,
with the speedometer laughing
past 60. What was I thinking
to let you sign on to dorm rooms
with, undoubtedly, marijuana
and hormonal boys and bisexual girls

Why didn't I raise you
Amish or Orthodox or
at least right wing?
Can I do this course over?
This is like the nightmares
where I get to school naked
and there's a final exam
two weeks early

You came back from the doctor's
with your booklet about
STDs something terribly dreadful
a month long sample
of birth control pills
and a prescription.
The room turned around
like that pill dispenser
I got dizzy.
I got tired.
I thought we'd discussed this:
no pills. Grandmom died of breast cancer.
I had my tumor carved out.
You calmly recited the risks:
stroke, cancer, blood clots…

I confiscated the pills, and the prescription
I let you keep the car keys.
I went to get coffee,

having aged ten years
in ten minutes

How do I let go
of my child?
I know less about doing this
than I knew about bringing you
into this world. ❧

Large

The truth is I am
large. I lament this.
Yet at forty-seven it's time
to make peace with my inner fat.

Mid-riff bulges into all
my space like an unwanted
younger sibling, with a life
of her own.

In America fat women
are only partially excused by
motherhood, kindness,
or an operatic voice.

Largeness is akin to
lethargy; among adolescents
and some honest adults
it is leprosy. ❧

Sunday, June 22, 1997

Mess of mail
stacked on my desk
accusing of errands undone,
affairs out of order.

A two year old statement from
Travelers Insurance that
settled an account.
Then you were walking, still,
remembering when to eat lunch

May 1996 newsletter left
where I dropped it a year ago
as your hair fell out and
the doctor insisted on a wheelchair
and we rented the hospital bed
for the playroom

The managed care directives
in August, undigested
as the hospice aide trained me
to roll you gently from side
to side, your eyes, so sweet
despite all you had seen,
smiling as the children sat beside
Your bed

Even that month
the companies sent their news
as if it mattered
as your eyes eased away
and we watched you depart,
your breath sawing through us
with sharp, serrated edges

So why is it a challenge
to file the letters
as if it mattered
what name I give the file
as if I could err and lose a paper
as if it mattered

And then in late August
the cancer that killed you
came back for me. I gripped
the chair and opened
the mail and stacked it up
while my friends fed my children
and I watched my own hair
fall into my fingers,
red drugs killed my blood cells
to save me.

Some day I'll end up
A paper on someone's desk;

A certificate of death
And it will matter to someone

But probably not the person
Who owns the desk. ✸

My Father Aaron's Words

Through the years I learned that words
would save me. When I was four,
brain cancer killed my father, but left his books.
He'd arrived in New York, 37 years old,
with wife, diplomas, bits of English. Here he
    learned more
by reading, searching, writing definitions in margins.

When I was ten I discovered the books.
With wet, trembling fingers I touched his words,
summoned his soul from the margins;
yet my prayers drew only silence of more
mute pages that turned and turned as they
    had before;
away, from my burning gut, so tangled with old

yearnings. I'd grown up watching who had more:
lovely father-creatures who spoke deep-voiced words,
and knew to fix things, knew wrenches were
    for turning
bolts to erect eternal shelves for books;
men who would live till gray and old,
to keep their families inside the margins.

Yet, still, my life was saved by words:
"Man Without a Country," marched across his book
that dwelled, unread, in my drawer, messenger for
my father, who'd lived outside the margins,
stateless through years of war, his old
school, shul, town, destroyed, no more.

And over the years I lost his books.
But memory held his writing in the margins.
Though time erased the actual words,
I breathed his love of learning more, more
words, more meanings, endless spells for
inner landscapes only dreamed or eons old.

Now at 48 I've lived one year more
than did my father. When cancer came for
me, the doctor excised it, with margins
enough to hope I'd grow old, old
enough to read grandchildren books,
to fill their ears with springs of words.

Words endure outside the margins
of time. Newborn, or old as brimstone, before
words were books, they were souls, they were more. ✑

THE FIRE IN ROB'S OFFICE

The pavement outside is soaked
and spent beneath the weight
of water that falls and falls
without end.

Small gray birds huddle on
the window sill, still
and peering in
from the rain
into the office.

Mother birds fuss and kiss
their babies' fallen feathers:
two-legged, four-legged,
wingless birds and
fathers who can't find food

they watch and wait
for the rain to end

and inside the work
of bloodless wounds and
hurts that shape the
bodies in the room
and steal the air

Somewhere,
sometimes, here
is the fire of healing. It
eats up pain and
lets out light.
The birds await, not fooled
by fancy words
they feel the heat
the air inside the office
where pain meets care. ❧

CANCER; WITH COMMUNITY

This journey unasked for:
waters loud and shaking.
   I stay afloat in tayva*
woven with get well notes
   and casseroles;
ribbons round a luscious rose
and wrapped about a text of poems.
   Messages left like medicine
   on my answering machine:
   "Found a joke"
   "Bringing miso"
   "Just a word to say hello"…

The waters will whiten,
wash all sins and sobbing,
then wane.
Even with body broken
my soul is whole.

I know
the crocus will grow
to kiss the snow,
and I will walk barefoot
on the grass
again. ❧

tayva: a word used only in two instances in the Torah. Once as Noah's "ark," then as the basket that held Moses.

THE ALEXANDER LESSON, AFTER AUSCHWITZ

My teacher is dressed in a pink shell
    and floral jumper.
    Tall ceilings and silent wood floor
The rooms filled with sturdy toys neatly stored
    and photos plainly framed.

"Free your neck," she says, soft and gentle.
    I aim to feel the innards of my neck
    like a blind woman seeking the door
    at the end of a hall

While a window opens from nowhere
    and through it I see
    the bodies hanging by the ropes
    watched by their loved ones
    starved and dazed and dying

Dangling like half-uttered questions
    asked of G-d
    interrupted and unanswered.

Fingers tap the hollow
    atop my spine.
    I wonder if they knew
    to free their neck,
    as they went up, up.
I wonder if that would have helped
    to release their wounded heads
    to the winds. ❧

BIOLOGICAL CLOCK 9/30/02

Years ago, the clock ticked, too. My eggs banged
at my belly, like toddlers waking from
naps, torsos thrusting at crib rails they longed
to flee. So one by one, my daughter and son

spilled forth to crawl and whirl, dance and twirl their
vibrance through the wake and sleep of light.
They grew. She off to college; he taller
than me. I forgot the clock. Till one night

the tick tock awoke to click my knee while
I climbed the stairs to my sleep, past her room,
her trophies and graffiti performed still.
Past my son's door, shut tight around his womb
of books and bass guitars, I am alone
though blessed by my husband's love, yet fingers
of time that squeeze my breath and my bones
demand to know why bother to linger?

With children now gone forth, will seconds now
just drone on, bored, no reason to hurry,
or will they drum a new rhythm, bestow
on my days unforeseen purpose, untold story. ❧

BIOLOGICAL CLOCK 11/26/02

Years past, that clock ticked, too. My eggs banged at
my belly, like toddlers waking from
their naps, their torsos thrust at cribs they longed
to flee. So one by one, my daughter and son

spilled forth to crawl and whirl, to dance and twirl
their vibrance through the wake and sleep of light.
They grew. She bounded off to college; he taller
than me. The clock forgotten. Till one night

the clock awoke and sent its hands to poke
through all my bones. A fever burned until
I, stunned, allowed the scans, the tests that showed
disease that had no cure. The doctor spoke:
You could have months, or years, or decades still.
I pray: to live with joy all time allowed. ∞

My Feet

I finally found my feet
Before I realized that I hadn't known them.

Humble twins content with soft socks and
    wiggle room,
All these years they've scurried about
Like foreign chauffeurs with thick accents
Carrying me everywhere.

Close to the soil, they know
The grandeur of groundedness,
The lightness lifting me into flight. ✒

Shore's Edge

Life and illness inspire this
August afternoon on my deck;
above the garden, beneath the maples,
amidst my playthings.

I write, as years ago, my toddlers
had played at the beach,
digging sand with purple shovels,
chartreuse buckets, and glee.

My toys:
pads of college-ruled paper;
wide red dictionary seemingly serene
but secretly thrilled to know I will swim
    its salty depths;
bold yellow pencils already etching paths
on pages with phrases and commas
and question marks.

I heal,
even as death advances
at an unknown pace;
the Holy One opens Her lamp
to hold me in a sunny gaze.

I kneel on a cushioned rug, and build
a poem; press sea-washed nouns into
watery sounds; mold messes of verbs
and descriptors into a castle of words

whose shape will hold till night awakens,
this deck darkens, and tidal swells
swallow all towers, moats,
    stranded words,
and me.

And then,
I pray,
the waters
will savor my soul,
and the sea, I pray,
will remember me. ❧

UNDERGROUND

Hurtling through the Metro,
D.C. 2003,
5764;
two timelines entwined.

This vessel impels us,
this impulse of motion,
emotion, motivation,
on cascading waves of
an ocean unseen
amid shores of concrete.

And then in the din, in the drone
of the bones of these caverns,
I hear as a heartbeat
contracting, expanding,
its essence arises,
descends, ever into
this sea; I

> *Hear O Israel*
> *The Lord our G-d*
> *The Lord is One*

Exhaled of all innards
I hear and then listen,
mystified at dissonance,
the difference, the union
of hearing and listening;
I only can breathe,

Feel the awe swim out
transcend clutter, debris,
and only that name that
announces itself in
this instant, incessant,
and yet, in a minute

we've reached our stop. ❧

STAGE IV: BREAST CANCER

I star tonight in the Big Tent
under the lights.
How I captivate the crowd!

My clown smile cradles tears
as I quiver on a unicycle
till collapse—
then rise in courage
to audience applause.

So adored!
As I speed around the arena,
my johnny flaps frantic farewells
to the acts left forever behind.

Ahead of schedule
the curtain drops.
I hurry to curtsey.
The onlookers cheer—

then
exit,
eager for the halos
at their bedside lamps—

envied by my lesions
burning
through
black
heaven.

TRANSFERRING EDDIE'S HOURS

I'd listened for years:
Dad had drowned on an August beach,
Mom then threatened their fractured home.
Eddie's booze, cocaine, the black dog.
Sobriety, degree, job, woman, child.

Tests, lapses, moving on.
Hour beyond hour I'd held
a steady mirror to his boyish cheeks
and budding heart, those eyes
that desired tomorrow—

Till today, and my disclosure:
"Unfortunately, my diagnosis
is serious and uncertain.
And so we must find you another
therapist with more hours."

After quiet, he replied,
"Will you have more hours, later?"

Truth ruptured.
My jaws spasmed, my eyes spit.
I'm sorry, I didn't mean this
to happen, the quiver of lips,
the tissues.

I never meant this,
to have holes in my
spine, my hold,
my hours. ❧

BONE BOX

The coffin will be simple
And pine; it will whisper
of deep forests silhouetted
on the sun's outstretched
arms. It will cradle me
with lullabies of twinkling
stars and rising moons.

How tidy: a box to
keep my bones compact,
beneath the soil,
beneath the walkway
with its other stones
holding the names
of bones buried here
along this path
or that lane.

My husband says he'll
bring stones from journeys
he'll make. Will we stay
connected through the
veil of body and spirit?

Perhaps my daughter will
bring her new man, her
babies; my son might
talk to me there,
the words that swim
within him.

Bone box, bone box. ❧

For Sue, on Losing Don

As I ride to the church,
the homes and villages glide by
as if
it were just another day.

But I only imagine
how the days have lost their breath
for you
every moment and photo and song
is irrevocably changed
and impossibly the same

How everyday might lose its rhyme and meter
for longer than one can bear.

And yet faith assures us
that just as the seeds you planted and fed
will find their way to bloom
and tickle the eager fingers of
Olivia and Jack,

so will the ancient seasons
teach you a new way
to wake and work and sleep and play,

and Don will gaze down,
his blue eyes shining with pride,
from Heaven. ❧

POST DIAGNOSIS

I did not expect to find these poems
strewn all over my world:
behind the front door in a dust ball,
growing green in a window sill planter,
tangled with hair in the bathroom sink.

Yet as the sun falls down,
these words appear in varying states
of deliverance and disrepair
and I cast up my nets to collect them
before I die. ☙

AFTERWORD

Compiling this collection brought me closer to my mother's poetry than I ever came during her lifetime. This might sound strange, since my mother and I were always close. My father used to shake his head in amazement at how much we could talk—at midnight over cereal during one of our many concurrent bouts of insomnia; in the backseat of the car on the way to grandparents in Queens or upstate New York; even, or perhaps especially, when I left for college. I remember hours spent almost every day, curled up in the chair with my shoulder hugging the phone to my ear, the first two awkward sentences of a paper I needed to write glaring at me from the computer screen. I've forgotten which of those conversations over the years led to the discovery that my mother and I had independently invented the same metaphor to describe the relationship between god and religion. We both preferred chewing an entire pack of gum at a time to just one piece—my mother joked that it was a tastier version of chain smoking. We even looked alike. I grew so used to being called "Laura" that I still turn around sometimes when I hear the name, wondering if someone is talking to me.

Thus I knew about my mother's passion for writing as I grew up. I knew, for example, that she met regularly with three women for "writer's group," though my understanding of the content of those meetings was shrouded in vagueness. Sometimes, on Yom Ha'Shoah, my mother's poetry would appear in the leaflet for the memorial service at my synagogue. I have distinct memories of standing in the Holocaust memorial garden, shivering and cradling the fragile flame of my yahrzeit candle against the wind of the falling April night, as I watched my mother step to the podium. She read one of her poems, her tone soft as though the words needed to be handled delicately, strong as though the words barely contained a potent force within her, something burning, blooming out of sight. As she spoke, I shifted from one foot to another, trying not to look up at the figure standing quietly before the microphone.

My discomfort stemmed from more than the un-remarkable embarrassment of a preteen daughter about her mother. I rarely read and even avoided her poetry until the last months of her life. By then,

Laura and her husband, Rob.

the endless cycle of illness and treatment had persuaded her to close her practice as a social worker, and my mother mentioned more than once during our regular phone rituals that "It's so nice to have time to just work on my writing." During Thanksgiving break that year, I found her hesitantly pressing a manila folder into my hands. I flipped through the pages inside, neatly typed, the crisp edges nearly untouched. "That's all I've managed to get together," my mother said. "I'm finally going to try and publish some of them." She paused, and added, "I've always been a little intimidated at showing you my poetry, for some reason…"

I felt intimidated at the thought of reading it. My mother laughed so loudly during my high school plays that even from backstage I could pick the sound of it from the crowd; she giggled when we made cranberry sauce because she liked to watch the berries pop; she could tell when I needed a good cry from the tone of my voice. These qualities, so warm and reassuring and connected to me, seemed alien to the world her poetry described. "Ugly smells curl out from safe looking places," the poems told me. "For me, all joy sheds tears," they confessed. I did not recognize these demons. I managed to read the first ten poems, really reading, not just skimming, never saying "how nice," as I turned a page. But I did not really understand how to fit the pieces together.

I read more and more as time went on: December with the seizure and the rattling midnight phone calls; January when I felt the world constricting to fit within the four walls of our house, within spans of time between compartments of the pill box; February when I learned how to hook up IV tubes and read aloud to my mother as she had once read

Alice in Wonderland to me. Despite not really know-ing where to place them, I shed my discomfort with her poems. Perhaps the illness made that burning, blooming force I caught sight of at Yom Ha'Shoah services less unnerving and more a fact of life. My father once compared watching my mother die to watching the wilting of a brilliant flower. I always thought of it as a peeling back of layers that time and trial had cocooned around the soul, until one glimpsed the vanishing flicker of the raw spark beneath. My mother and I talked less often about shopping, weight, politics. More often than we ever had, curled up together with the pages spread around us on her bed, we read her poetry.

Even after the funeral, I kept stumbling across her poems, left tucked away in unlikely places. My father, brother and I found them in her files in between outdated tax forms, or in notebooks left on bookshelves throughout the house, or in boxes in the attic among letters from her middle school friends. In a similar manner we unearthed an old photograph from her college years that now looks out at us from the mantle piece. In the picture, my mother grins in black-and-white, her eyes wide and laughing, tongue sticking out at whoever held the camera. My father says that it's his favorite photo of her. "Your mother had a lot of intense feelings, you know," he said once, contemplating it. "But somehow she always knew how to be silly."

His words stay with me as I read her poetry now. Once, her poems had filled me with a feeling of vertigo, of tumbling from the safety of her presence into unfamiliar depths. Now I stare into the pages, trying to catch a glimpse of the fingers around the pencil, the wrist brushing the page, a hint of those warm, reassuring layers that had once seemed so outside these words. I still look eagerly for traces of her handwriting when I fumble through papers in the filing cabinet or on her desk. Finding it, reading it for the first time, feels almost like finding another conversation.

The discovery of those long-lost poems might be evidence for the desire to conceal some mysterious

inner reality. One might then find the irreconcilable incongruity that I once found. I think of the found poems as gemstones, glowing slightly among the mundane where they had been scattered, giving color to those ordinary corners we all took for granted. I often pause on my way past my father's favorite photograph, thinking of how deep her joy must have run, to carry all the heaviness of her poems up into that smile. "Spirits sing/in sadness, inside me, incessantly—" my mother wrote once. "Delight!/in the forest/in our memory/You will find a true path!/...I pray for cleansing,/purity of purpose;/I cross the stream."

Anna Cable

To order more copies, send $10.00 plus $5.00 for shipping and handling to:

Temple Emanuel Gift Shop
99 Taft Avenue
Providence, RI 02906

Proceeds from the sale of this book will go to The Chakrin Cable Family Youth Fund at Temple Emanuel.